NURSERY RHYMES

Mother Goose

MOTHER GOOSE RHYMES

Friendly Faces

PEOPLE NURSERY RHYMES

compiled by Terry Pierce ✺ illustrated by Fernando Luiz

PICTURE WINDOW BOOKS
Minneapolis, Minnesota

Special thanks to our advisers for their expertise:

Terry Flaherty, Ph.D., Professor of English
Minnesota State University, Mankato

Susan Kesselring, M.A., Literacy Educator
Rosemount–Apple Valley–Eagan (Minnesota) School District

Editors: Christianne Jones and Dodie Marie Miller
Designer: Tracy Davies
Page Production: Angela Kilmer
Art Director: Nathan Gassman
The illustrations in this book were created digitally.

Editor's Note: Editorial and formatting decisions for most
of the nursery rhymes in this book were based on the
following source: *The Random House Book of Mother
Goose* (1986), selected and illustrated by Arnold Lobel.

Picture Window Books
5115 Excelsior Boulevard
Suite 232
Minneapolis, MN 55416
877-845-8392
www.picturewindowbooks.com

Library of Congress Cataloging-in-Publication Data
Pierce, Terry.
Friendly faces : people nursery rhymes / compiled by Terry
Pierce ; illustrated by Fernando Luiz.
p. cm. – (Mother Goose rhymes)
Summary: An illustrated collection of twenty nursery
rhymes about people.
ISBN-13: 978-1-4048-2349-5 (library binding)
ISBN-10: 1-4048-2349-2 (library binding)
ISBN-13: 978-1-4048-2355-6 (paperback)
ISBN-10: 1-4048-2355-7 (paperback)
1. Nursery rhymes. 2. Human beings–Juvenile poetry.
3. Children's poetry. [1. Nursery rhymes. 2. Human
beings–Poetry.] I. Luiz, Fernando, ill. II. Mother Goose.
Selections. III. Title. IV. Title: People nursery rhymes.
PZ8.3.P558643Fri 2006
398.3–dc22 [E]   2006027243

TABLE OF CONTENTS

MOTHER GOO

NURSERY RHYMES ABOUT PEOPLE

Many nursery rhymes are about people with popular names like Mary, Jack, or John. Nursery rhymes also tell us things that people did long ago. They tell us what they ate, the games they played, and how they worked. Who is your favorite rhyme about? Maybe you can find a rhyme with your name in it.

LITTLE MISS MUFFET

Little Miss Muffet
Sat on a tuffet
Eating her curds and whey;
There came a big spider,
Who sat down beside her
And frightened Miss Muffet away.

JACK AND JILL

Jack and Jill went up the hill
To fetch a pail of water;
Jack fell down and broke his crown,
And Jill came tumbling after.

JACK BE NIMBLE

Jack be nimble,
Jack be quick,
Jack jump over
The candlestick.

LITTLE BO-PEEP

Little Bo-Peep has lost her sheep
And doesn't know where to find them;
Leave them alone, and they'll come home,
Bringing their tails behind them.

MARY HAD A LITTLE LAMB

Mary had a little lamb,
Its fleece was white as snow;
And everywhere that Mary went
The lamb was sure to go.

It followed her to school one day,
That was against the rule;
It made the children laugh and play
To see a lamb in school.

And so the teacher turned it out,
But still it lingered near
And waited patiently about
Till Mary did appear.

Why does the lamb love Mary so?
The eager children cry;
Why, Mary loves the lamb, you know,
The teacher did reply.

OLD MOTHER HUBBARD

Old Mother Hubbard
Went to the cupboard
To fetch her poor dog a bone;
But when she came there
The cupboard was bare
And so the poor dog had none.

∾ HUMPTY DUMPTY ∾

Humpty Dumpty sat on a wall,
Humpty Dumpty had a great fall;
All the king's horses and all the king's men
Couldn't put Humpty together again.

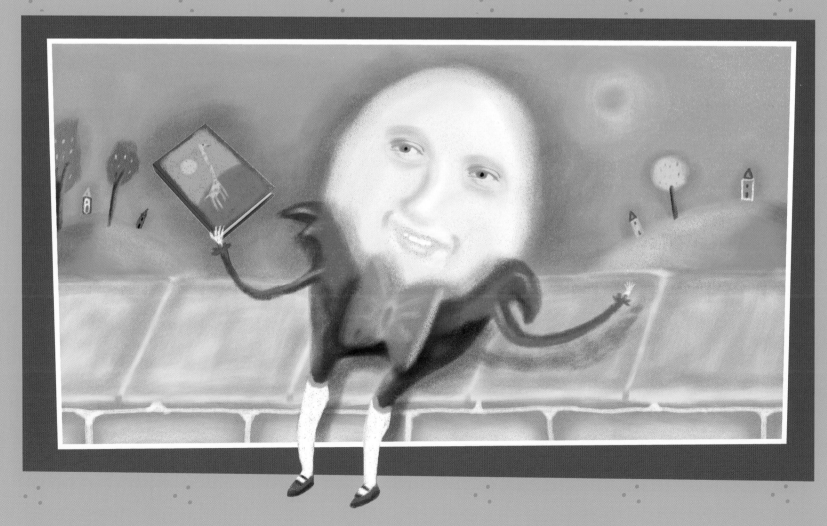

LITTLE JACK HORNER

Little Jack Horner
Sat in a corner,
Eating a Christmas pie;
He put in his thumb
And pulled out a plum
And said, "What a good boy am I."

YANKEE DOODLE

Yankee Doodle went to town,
Riding on a pony.
He stuck a feather in his hat
And called it macaroni.

BETTY BOTTER

Betty Botter bought some butter,
But, she said, the butter's bitter;
If I put it in my batter,
It will make my batter bitter,
But a bit of better butter
Will make my batter better.
So she bought a bit of butter,
Better than her bitter butter,
And she put it in her batter
And the batter was not bitter.
So it was better Betty Botter bought
A bit of better butter.

MARY, MARY, QUITE CONTRARY

Mary, Mary, quite contrary,
How does your garden grow?
With silver bells and cockleshells,
And pretty maids all in a row.

LITTLE TOMMY TUCKER

Little Tommy Tucker
Sings for his supper:
What shall we give him?
White bread and butter.
How shall he cut it
Without even a knife?
How will he be married
Without even a wife?

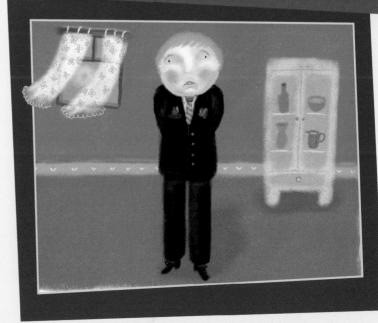

OLD KING COLE

Old King Cole
Was a merry old soul,
And a merry old soul was he;
He called for his pipe,
And he called for his bowl,
And he called for his fiddlers three.

Every fiddler, he had a fiddle,
And a very fine fiddle had he;
Twee tweedle dee, tweedle dee,
Went the fiddlers.
Oh, there's none so rare
As can compare
With King Cole and his fiddlers three.

PETER PIPER

Peter Piper picked a peck of pickled peppers;
A peck of pickled peppers Peter Piper picked;
If Peter Piper picked a peck of pickled peppers,
Where's the peck of pickled peppers Peter Piper picked?

HANDY-SPANDY, JACK-A-DANDY

Handy-spandy,
Jack-a-Dandy,
Loves plum cake
And sugar candy.
He bought some
At a grocer's shop,
And out he came,
Hop, hop, hop, hop.

23

~ GEORGIE PORGIE ~

Georgie Porgie, pudding and pie,
Kissed the girls and made them cry;
When the boys came out to play,
Georgie Porgie ran away.

SIMPLE SIMON

Simple Simon met a pieman
Going to the fair;
Says Simple Simon to the pieman,
Let me taste your ware.

THE GRAND OLD DUKE OF YORK

The grand old Duke of York he had ten thousand men
He marched them up to the top of the hill
And he marched them down again.

And when they were up, they were up
And when they were down, they were down
But when they were only halfway up
They were neither up nor down.

LUCY LOCKET LOST HER POCKET

Lucy Locket lost her pocket,
Kitty Fisher found it;
Not a penny was there in it,
Only ribbon round it.

OLD MOTHER GOOSE

Old Mother Goose,
When she wanted to wander,
Would ride through the air
On a very fine gander.

And Old Mother Goose
The goose saddled soon,
And mounting its back,
Flew up to the moon.

THE HISTORY OF NURSERY RHYMES AND
MOTHER GOOSE

Nursery rhymes circulated orally for hundreds of years. In the 18th century, collectors wrote down the rhymes, printed them, and sold them to parents and other adults to help them remember the rhymes so they could share them with children.

Some of these collections were called "Mother Goose" collections. Nobody knows exactly who Mother Goose was (though there are plenty of myths about her), but she was probably a respected storyteller. Occasionally the rhymes commented on real people and events. The meaning of many of the rhymes has been lost, but the catchy rhythms remain.

Mother Goose nursery rhymes have evolved from many sources through time. From the 1600s until now, the appealing rhythms, rhymes, humor, and playfulness found in these verses, stories, and concepts contribute to what readers now know as Mother Goose nursery rhymes.

TO LEARN MORE

AT THE LIBRARY

Delcher, Eden A. *Rhymes About Children.* Baltimore: Allan Publishers, 1992.

Finch, Mary. *Playtime Rhymes for Little People.* Cambridge, Mass.: Barefoot Books, 2006.

Hopkins, Lee Bennett. *People from Mother Goose: A Question Book.* San Diego: Harcourt Brace Jovanovich, 1989.

ON THE WEB

FactHound offers a safe, fun way to find Web sites related to this book. All of the sites on FactHound have been researched by our staff.

1. Visit *www.facthound.com*
2. Type in this special code: 1404823492
3. Click on the FETCH IT button.

Your trusty FactHound will fetch the best sites for you!

INDEX OF FIRST LINES

∽ LOOK FOR ALL OF THE BOOKS IN THE ∽ MOTHER GOOSE RHYMES SERIES:

Counting Your Way: Number Nursery Rhymes

Cuddly Critters: Animal Nursery Rhymes

Forecasting Fun: Weather Nursery Rhymes

Friendly Faces: People Nursery Rhymes

Sleepytime: Bedtime Nursery Rhymes

Ticktock: Time Nursery Rhymes

Mother Goose

NURSERY RHYMES